CW00890719

Bodybuilders

small group bible resources

Designed for great things

wrestling with human nature

Anton Baumohl

Scripture Union, 207–209 Queensway, Bletchley, MK2 2EB, England.
Email:info@scriptureunion.org.uk
www.scriptureunion.org.uk

Scripture Union Australia, Locked Bag 2, Central Coast Business Centre, NSW 2252

Small Group Resources, 1 Hilton Place, Harehills, Leeds, LS8 4HE

Note: *Designed for Great Things* was originally published under the title *How Human Can You Get?*

ISBN 1 85999 585 3

British Library Cataloguing-in-Publication Data
A catalogue record for this book is available from the British Library.

Cover design by David Lund Design
Internal page design by David Lund Design
Internal page layout by Mac Style Ltd, Scarborough, N. Yorkshire

Printed and bound in Great Britain by Ebenezer Baylis & Son Ltd, The Trinity Press, London Road, Worcester WR5 2JH

Introducing Bodybuilders

 **ORIGINS AND APPROACH**

BODYBUILDERS resources have a strong emphasis on building relationships, helping groups discover the real meaning of **koinonia** – the loving fellowship of Christian believers within which people really care for one another. Group members are encouraged to apply God's Word in ways that produce action and change – all within a secure, supportive atmosphere.

This relational approach to small group experience was first developed in the US by author Lyman Coleman under the title *Serendipity*. In the 1980s Scripture Union, in partnership with another publisher, *Small Group Resources*, took that as the foundation of nine studies under the *Serendipity* branding specially written for the UK market.

This **BODYBUILDERS** series recognises the value and strength of the *Serendipity* approach and contains much of the original material. In a sense, homegroups of the early 21st century may be far more ready to adopt this relational approach than their predecessors. Home groups have moved on; expectations have changed. Revisions and extra new material reflect that progress and also make the series pioneering in the sense of providing a more complete off-the-shelf package.

Christians are not immune from the pressures of society – stresses in the home, workplace, college, places of social interaction. When questioned, most people admit to a deep need for security, a sense

of belonging, and a safe environment in which to share themselves and be given support. Many are dissatisfied with the superficial relationships that often characterise contemporary living. They identify lonely chasms in their inner beings, empty of meaningful relationships. They long for practical ways in which to work out their heart commitment to Jesus Christ.

Central to the approach is an understanding that satisfying relationships can be nurtured in small groups in dynamic ways when people are prepared to take risks in opening themselves up to God and to each other. This shared vulnerability works within four contexts:

- **storytelling**
- **affirmation**
- **goal setting**
- **koinonia**

People need to share themselves and need to hear others sharing their own lives for relationships to grow. This is **storytelling**. Everyone needs to be listened to. When we respond to someone with a 'thank you', or 'I found your contribution helpful', we demonstrate that they are valuable and have a contribution to make to the growth of others. This is **affirmation**. Experiencing this in a group that meets regularly – even over a limited time – people begin to share their deeper longings or hurts, discovering that they can trust others for support in their struggles. Individuals can listen for what God is saying to them and implement changes – **goal setting** within the security of **koinonia**. BODYBUILDERS encourage all these stages to be reached through Bible study.

MEETING NEEDS IN CHURCHES AND COMMUNITIES

BODYBUILDERS aim to meet:

- **the need for applied biblical knowledge** – Christians are crying out for help in applying their faith in a confusingly complex world. Knowing what the Bible says isn't enough; people want to know how to translate knowledge into action.
- **the need to belong** – increasing pressures, accelerating pace of life, constant change: these work against committed relationships, which many feel should be a distinctive feature of the local church as it witnesses to a lonely generation.
- **the need to share the burden** – pressures on Christians are often intolerable, as demonstrated by emotional/ psychological disorders, increasing divorce rates, and the problems of ineffective parenting. One answer is for Christians to take seriously the sharing of each others' burdens – not only prayerfully but practically.
- **the need to build the church as community** – there is a growing conviction that the church should be a community living out the true nature of God's kingdom, experiencing New Testament koinonia.

BODYBUILDERS IN PRACTICE

Using BODYBUILDERS to form new groups: The ideal size for a group is between five and 12, meeting in a home or a church. Newcomers can be added into the group at any time, but care should be taken to give them a thorough briefing on 'the story so far'. The particular purposes of the group in growing relationships and discovering how to apply Bible truths to everyday life need to be made plain.

Using BODYBUILDERS in established groups: This material differs from much on the market to resource small groups. Make sure from the outset that the group appreciates that it is more interactive and, in some ways, more demanding. There is an emphasis on application as well as understanding.

Leading the BODYBUILDERS Group: If belonging to this group can be demanding, leading it is more so! The leader needs to have thought about the **BODYBUILDERS** approach and the goals. Ideally, there needs to be knowledge of the group, too, so that the material can be adapted to meet their particular needs. Options are given, and it is the leader who decides which and how much of that material is appropriate. Bearing in mind the emphasis on relationship building, the leader must ensure the group does not become a 'clique', too inward-looking or isolated. The leader makes sure everyone has a chance to speak, assisting those who find contributing difficult. He or she may need to take the initiative in promoting relationship building, which might include practical things like providing lists of telephone numbers, encouraging lift sharing, even organising a baby-sitting rota, as well as exercising pastoral care and leadership.

Each group member needs to feel committed to building relationships and willing to share personally. Regular attendance is a priority. Members aim to make themselves available to each other. Make sure everyone knows that there is complete confidentiality in respect of all that is shared. Encourage prayer for each other between meetings – and set an example yourself.

Practically speaking, you will need plenty of pens and large sheets of plain paper, and sometimes supplies of felt-tip pens, scissors, glue and old magazines or newspapers. Some Icebreakers need pre-prepared visual aids, or even some re-arrangement of furniture! Look ahead to plan for the coming sessions.

All the booklets in this series, each self-contained, contain material for six sessions. Some groups may want to add an introductory evening to explain the **BODYBUILDERS** approach, perhaps in a social setting over a pot-luck meal. The material can be worked through at a slower pace, if that is preferred.

Most of the interactive material is confined to a double-page spread for each session, so that the leader can photocopy it as an A4 sheet to be given out. Alternatively, everyone can have their own copy of the book. Make sure you allow people enough time to jot down answers on their response sheets. Ring the changes: sometimes it's helpful for people to complete responses in twos or threes, especially when a little discussion time is appropriate.

Variety and freedom are hallmarks of the **BODYBUILDERS** material. Leaders can select from the material to put together each session's programme:

Prayer/ Worship (variable time) – options are given, so that you can tailor your selection to whatever your group feels most comfortable with. Hymns and songs suggested are drawn from several popular collections currently on the market published by Kingsway: various editions *of Songs and Hymns of Fellowship, Spring Harvest Praise*, *New Songs* and *Stoneleigh* and *The Source*. Your group may be more comfortable with songs from other traditions. It is always helpful, though, to try to match songs to the theme.

Icebreaker (15 minutes) – this warm-up session is intended to relax the group and focus them on being together, and is usually based on the theme.

Relational Bible study (15 minutes) – this is an initial, fairly light excursion into the Bible verses, relating them to the lives of those in the group through multiple choice questions. If the group is large or time is limited, it may be that not everyone shares every question. By the way, Bible verses quoted in **BODYBUILDERS** almost always come from the NIV (New International Version), but you can use another translation. Often it's helpful to have a selection of different translations to compare when studying a particular passage.

In Depth (20 minutes) – moving deeper into the Bible verses, discovering more about their relationship to life.

My story (10–20 minutes) – an encouragement for people to relate teaching to everyday lives.

Going further (15 minutes) – this often involves other parts of the Bible containing similar teaching. If not used during group time, this can be taken away for further personal study during the week.

Enjoy! Discover! Grow!

IN THE SAME SERIES ...

BODYBUILDERS

small group Bible resources

Relationship Building – growing a caring and committed community
Lance Pierson

It's impossible to live daily life without constant interaction with the people around us: family, neighbours, friends or workmates. These six sessions will help you and your group develop the skills needed to build healthy relationships.
ISBN 1 85999 582 9

Growing through change – seizing the opportunities life gives you
Lance Pierson

Do we fear change because we have mis-placed our emotional security? These six sessions challenge you and your group to find security in God himself, to welcome any kind of change as an opportunity to deepen that trust, and to discover strength and support in the community of the church.
ISBN 1 85999 585 7

Living for the King – growing God's rule in our world
'Tricia Williams

'God in control? It doesn't look like it!' Is that your reaction to the suffering and injustice you see in the world? These six sessions look at key issues which have immediate relevance for those who want to be involved in the risky and exciting business of being God's community here and now.
ISBN 1 85999 584 5

Surviving under pressure – finding strength in the tough times
Christopher Griffiths & Stephen Hathway

We live in high-pressure days, bombarded with conflicting views and influences that can be obstacles to adopting lifestyles that truly reflect Christian values and principles. These six sessions are aimed at equipping Christian believers to stand firm even on the roughest ground.
ISBN 1 85999 585 X

A Fresh Encounter – meeting the real Jesus
David Bolster

Some were intrigued, attracted to him, accepted, loved and followed him; others were afraid of him, were disturbed by him or rejected him. These six sessions challenge you and your group to extend your understanding of who Jesus is and what that means in everyday life.
ISBN 1 85999 586 1

Available from all good Christian bookshops or from Scripture Union Mail Order:
PO Box 5148, Milton Keynes MLO, MK2 2YX, Tel: 01908 856006
or online through www.scriptureunion.org.uk

DESIGNED FOR GREAT THINGS
– wrestling with human nature

INTRO

Almost everyone would agree that humanity is unique on this earth. Even those who have no belief in God might point to our advanced intelligence or to the moral dimension which sets us apart from the rest of the living world. It is impossible, however, to separate from this high view of humanity our ability to perpetrate the most inexplicable evil. Throughout history we have been the greatest destructive force on the earth – destroying the inanimate world, the living world of plants and animals, and indeed our own species as well.

Some would argue that humanity has it within itself to rectify all past evils, and ultimately to live in harmony with the rest of creation and to reach its full potential. There is little evidence of this actually happening.

It is only the Christian view of humanity that provides explanations that make sense of the reality we see around us. It is only the Christian view that can bring together the beautiful uniqueness and the destructive inclination. It is only the Christian view that can offer hope for the future of humanity that is consistent with what has happened in the past.

The Christian view is that we are:
- created sharing many aspects of God's nature, and therefore the highest form of animal life, of infinite value;
- fallen into rebellion against God's will, and therefore capable of monstrous evil;
- loved by God to the extent that Jesus, the one perfect Man, himself endured the penalty for the wrongdoing of all other people, as he died on the cross;
- capable, therefore, of receiving God's forgiveness, becoming God's children and growing further into God's likeness in this life;
- intended, as the extension of the above, to share God's glory in heaven.

Many studies on the Christian doctrine of humanity tend to jump from looking at sin and suffering in the present, to the hope of our future inheritance obtained through the death and resurrection of Jesus. In this series of studies we hope to linger a little longer on people as we were made, and as we exist now in this life. Sessions 1, 2 and 3 look at people as God's creation, people in God's image and people as God's children. Session 5 focuses on the potential for us in this world. Only in Sessions 4 and 6 do we come to people's sinful nature and future hope.

There *is* hope for all men and women – none are so evil that God cannot use or renew them. Even the non-Christian has something of the image of God still residing in him or her. After God, humanity is the next major theme in the Bible. We hope that through this study you will be challenged to see the positive things in yourself and in others around you, and know more of how to handle the negative things.

MADE TO ORDER

AIM: to explore what it means for men and women to be God's special creation, and how this should affect the way we view ourselves and our lives.

NOTES FOR LEADERS

It will be important to establish an atmosphere of warmth and trust in which people are encouraged to contribute and know that they will be valued for any contribution they make.

PRAYER/WORSHIP IDEAS

Songs and hymns

If this is a first meeting for the group, encourage members to be free to express themselves in worship in ways they find meaningful and to be accepting of the way others may choose to worship. Make clear that clapping or raising hands or arms, etc are acceptable (indeed, biblical!), as are different postures for prayer (kneeling, sitting, standing, etc).

If you have a musician in your group, ask them (in advance!) to come prepared to lead a time of sung worship. If you're without a musician, using a CD and providing the words for people to sing along is just as good. You might like to use songs such as the following in order to help the group focus on the idea of God as our Creator:

I the Lord of sea and sky
O Lord, my God (How great thou art)
We believe
I'm special
O God of love (How good it is)

Opening prayer

Try to gather together all the group's anticipation, excitement and maybe even apprehension at the prospect of the next few weeks – not just the subject matter under discussion but also the relationship building that will be happening.

During the meeting

Praying the words of Scripture back to God can be very powerful. Read Psalm 139 aloud around the group (each group member reading two or three verses). After a few moments for reflection, encourage them to pray (aloud if possible) something from the psalm. For example, 'Thank you God that you know me…', 'Thank you God that there is nowhere I can go where your Spirit will not be…', etc. You'll be amazed just how much food for thanksgiving and praise you find.

ICEBREAKER
How well do I know you?

If most folk in your group know each other a little, ask them to find a partner and spend three minutes telling him or her as much as they know about them. When the time is up, their partner should tell them whether all their information was correct or not and which parts were wrong. Then repeat the exercise with the other person.

Alternatively, and especially if all the people in your group are new, try an icebreaker called 'Flapping Fish' that's purely for fun! You will need: some floor space (preferably not carpeted); two 'fish' cut out of a single sheet of newspaper; two rolled-up whole newspapers.

Divide your team into two and give each a fish and a newspaper. The aim is for them to create a draught behind the fish and move it forward by flapping the newspaper on the floor behind it. Have a fixed point across the room which is the finishing line. The first players in each team must race to flap the fish over the line and back to the team, then the next player does the same, etc. The first team to finish is the winner.

BIBLE READING
Psalm 139

RELATIONAL BIBLE STUDY
The third question is most important here. Spend most of the time sharing how and why each participant feels the way they do. If you have a large group, divide into threes and fours for this.

IN DEPTH
It's the last question in this section that you should spend most time on; there are likely to be some who see only their spiritual nature as of interest to God. If people hold this view, point out the that Hebrew writers of the Bible had no such concept of man; they viewed man as an integrated whole, all of equal importance to God. If you want to major on Question 3, it may be worth omitting Question 2, or adding it to Going Further. People may find it harder than it looks, as some of the phrases in the left-hand column could arguably relate to more than one of the quotes in the psalm. There is potential for fruitful discussion here! For what it's worth, you can work out which phrase we think matches each quote by putting the quotes into verse order; they are then alongside their companion phrases.

MY STORY
Try to be sensitive to the people in your group. This section invites them to think about their attitudes to themselves. If your group is new or not used to sharing at this level, allow people the option of not sharing what they write down. They should feel free to just say 'pass' when it comes to their turn. Sharing of this nature should be done in groups of not more than four – another option is to share in pairs.
If the group finds Question 3 difficult, be prepared to lead off yourself – this is an ideal way of encouraging others. Thank God in whatever way you feel is most appropriate for your group – silence, open prayer, singing, a re-reading of Psalm 139.

GOING FURTHER

notes on the Bible verses

Psalm 139

Some commentators believe that this psalm or part of it was written by someone on the run from God (139:7–12). It certainly is a reflection of the impossibility of getting away from a God who knows his creation intimately. The psalm reflects the wonder of a writer who has discovered a God who knew all about him before he was even born! This psalm is both far-ranging in the ground it covers, and also intimate and personal.

139:1–6: God's knowledge of us is not just that of the cold, all-seeing eye; it is personal and warm and prompted by his intimate love for us. He knows us better than we know ourselves.

139:13–16: God's intimate knowledge stems from the fact that he was involved in our creation and formation. God created every dimension of human life and not just the spiritual. The Hebrews had no concept of a spiritual being separated from mind, body and emotion – all these formed an integral whole in their thinking.

139:19–24: The psalmist turns back from the heights to the reality of living in a fallen world. He sounds vindictive, but his indignation is against those who mar what God created good.

MADE TO ORDER

BIBLE READING
Psalm 139

RELATIONAL BIBLE STUDY

1 With what would you compare God's knowledge of you? Circle any appropriate letters.

a A car assembly line worker who has put it all together.
b A psychiatrist who has examined every corner of your mind.
c A mother who has watched and nurtured you all of your life.
d A beachcomber who has explored every grain of sand.
e A sculptor who moulded and smoothed every curve.
f A reconnaissance pilot using infra-red so that he can see even at night.
g Other:_____

2 How do you feel about God knowing you so well? Choose and circle the statement that best describes your feelings.

a afraid of someone with those powers
b embarrassed at being so visible
c ashamed that someone knows all your secrets
d relieved that God does not ignore you
e proud that the Creator of the universe knows you
f excited that you are part of God's master-plan
g Other: _____

IN DEPTH

1 Which of the following descriptions of mankind would this psalm challenge?

a Naked ape: little more than a highly developed animal.
b Social insect: organised in communities governed by sociological laws.
c Thinker: able to work out complex problems.
d God-like: controlling all the power and potential of the universe.
e Moral chooser: able to distinguish between right and wrong.
f Spiritual being: with a spiritual dimension to life.

2 People are the climax of God's creation. What makes men and women so special? Draw lines from the phrases on the left-hand column to the quote from the psalm you think it could be deduced from – each phrase illustrating something special about humanity.

a Can reason things out...   *Do I not hate those who hate you, O Lord... (v 21)*
b Is specially 'made to order' by God...   *I am fearfully and wonderfully made. (v 14)*
c Can feel emotions...   *Lead me in the way everlasting. (v 24)*
d Can know God   *For you created my inmost being; you knit me together... (v 13)*
e Can make moral choices   *...you perceive my thoughts from afar. (v 2)*
f Is potentially immortal   *How precious to me are your thoughts O God! (v17)*

3 God created every aspect of us. How much are you aware of the Creator's concern for and involvement in the different dimensions of your existence?

Put a cross on the line to indicate how aware you feel of God's concern for the areas of your life listed below. (You may decide that one of the extremes or the mid-point doesn't fit you exactly, so put your cross somewhere in between.)

	Very much aware	Never thought about it before	Completely unaware
a your physical body			
b your social relationships			
c your emotions/feelings			
d your spiritual being			
e your mind and mental powers			
f your personality			

MY STORY

I Which aspect of you do you feel at the moment most grateful to your Creator for making (body, mind, spirit, emotions, the ability to relate to people, etc)?

_____

2 Which one of the five aspects of your life listed in the last question would you like to share more fully with God?

_____

Think of up to three practical steps you could take in the next month to allow the Creator to become more involved in this area.

a _____
b _____
c _____

going further

I What biblical evidence can you find to illustrate that God created mankind as the following? (In each case the references are given as starters; use a concordance or other Bible reference book to help you find out more.)

a a spiritual being (Mark 12:28–30; John 4:24)

b a social being (Mark 12:28–31; Genesis 2:18–24; Numbers 1:1–19; Romans 12:4–10)

c an emotional being (Ecclesiastes 3:4; John 11:35–36; Romans 12:15)

d a physical being (Genesis 1:28–29; Genesis 2:7; Leviticus 11:1–23; 1 Corinthians 6:18–20):

e a thinking being (Romans 12:1–2; Genesis 2:19–20; Philippians 4:8)

2 The Bible has little to say about play, humour or fun. How would you argue that God intends fun to be a legitimate part of human experience?

3 God has plans for us before we are born, see Psalm 139:13–16. Are these verses sufficient to counter all arguments for abortion?

LIKE FATHER, LIKE SON

AIM: to explore what it means to be made 'in the image of God', and how that affects our relationship with the rest of creation.

NOTES FOR LEADERS

PRAYER/WORSHIP IDEAS

Songs and hymns
Either with an accompanying musician or CD and words, spend some time in worship. The following songs are ideas:

Praise him, you heavens
Let everything that has breath
Father of creation

During the meeting
Ask people to share a memory of a wonderful feature of creation and the impression it had on them. What did it tell them about God? For example, someone may have been to the Grand Canyon or to the French Alps on holiday and have been awed by what they saw. Spend a short time thanking God for his creation.

ICEBREAKER
Invite your group to draw their 'family character' on a sheet of blank paper. First everyone should make a list of the ways they are like parents and/or children – in looks and personality. Now convert the list into a number of simple drawings; for example, if you have the same nose, you might like to draw a picture of the nose (a physical feature). If you recognise their impatient temperament in you, you might draw a wiggly line to signify impatience (as a feature of personality). Share your 'family character' drawings with a partner; start by

trying to guess the meaning of each other's drawings – then share the right answers. If you have anyone in your group who did not grow up with parents and does not have children, invite them to think about the group of people to whom they are most close, and do a family likeness of them. Alternatively, they could describe the 'family character' of a family they know well.

RELATIONAL BIBLE STUDY

IN DEPTH
If you feel these questions are unlikely to raise any significant discussion in your group, plan to tackle at least one of the Going Further questions during your session. Question 2 in Going Further may be a particularly good one here, to promote deeper thought and discussion, leading to action.

MY STORY
The 'affirmation' exercises in Questions 2 and 3 may need careful introduction if your group is not used to this type of activity. Your job is to help people accept compliments gracefully with a 'thank you' (not rejecting them in false humility), and to ensure that no one is left out of sharing. If someone is so new to the group that they couldn't effectively take part in the exercise, suggest that they sit this one out and learn about others from the comments. Where this does happen, always bring that person back into the discussion at the end of the exercise by saying something like, 'Well, how did that seem to you, John? Did we all look comfortable hearing something nice about ourselves?'

GOING FURTHER
Make sure that any suggestions for group action in Question 3 are considered by the whole group at some stage.

Things to remember ...

notes on the Bible verses

 Genesis 1:26–31

1:26 *Man:* This is plural (see *them* referred to later) and means mankind or people in general. *Image, likeness:* this sets man apart from the rest of creation. In this particular passage the likeness is seen in:

- man's special responsibility for the rest of creation;
- man's ability to know God and understand God talking to him.

This likeness is seen in other characteristics as well, including the ability to make moral choices, to love, to reason, to commune with God. One

consequence of being special is that man is also accountable to God for his actions.

At the Fall, God's image was not destroyed in man; it was only marred. So today that image can still be seen to some extent in all human beings.

1:28 *Subdue, rule:* Man's charge is to look after (take care of and be responsible for) the rest of creation. This is an extension of God's work as Creator and Sustainer. It therefore has implications for how man should preserve the natural world, domesticate plants and animals, use them for his own purposes, and apply science and technology (see also Psalm 8:4–8).

LIKE FATHER, LIKE SON

BIBLE READING
Genesis 1:26–31

RELATIONAL BIBLE STUDY

1 How do you react when you look in the mirror in the morning? (Underline your most likely reaction.)

a 'Hello gorgeous!'
b 'I must do something about those wrinkles.'
c 'Ugh!'

d I never look in a mirror.
e 'It's what's on the inside that counts!'
f Other _____

2 How do you respond to your role as 'ruler' of the rest of the living world?

a I can't stand cats.
b Our pets seem to rule us!
c Leave it to the wildlife experts.
d Everything is specialised nowadays, and animals are the farmer's responsibility.
e I really haven't got time.

f I wouldn't know where to start.
g It's too late; we've ruined the world already.
h I try to keep the countryside green.
i Other _____
_____

3 'Subdue' the earth (1:28) means:

a Be tough and stop the rest of creation from getting out of line.
b Tend and cultivate it like a devoted gardener.
c Get rid of all weeds and disease-carrying insects.
d Domesticate the animals and grow the crops in fields.
e Multiply until you outnumber all other species..
f Other: _____

IN DEPTH

1 Why do you think God made man in his own image? (Circle as many as you feel are appropriate.)

a Because he is perfect and wanted to make something else perfect.
b Because he's vain.
c Because he wanted a creature to relate to at an intimate level.
d Because he was bored.
e We were an experiment!
f It was the natural progression in the line of creation.
g As an expression of his love.
h Other _____

2 What does being made in God's image (1:26,27) imply?

a God has hands and feet.
b Human beings are more than just molecules.
c Human beings share God's rule over the world of nature.

d God is both male and female.
e God has a wife.
f Human beings are able to think, choose and make.
g Human beings are able to love.
h Other _____

3 In what ways is man like God? (Circle any that apply.)

loving	supernatural	holy
good-looking	responsible	just
perfect	reasoning	moral
compassionate	vegetarian	powerful
immortal	wise	
able to form relationships		creative
can predict the future		Other?

MY STORY

I Do you recognise any of God's likeness in yourself? Humbly try to identify features from Question 4 of the In Depth section that you think you possess to some degree.

2 Look round the group, and try to identify something of God's image in each person you see. Write the qualities alongside the names of group members.

Name   The aspect of God's image that I see

_____

_____

_____

_____

3 God's image is in all people (not just Christians). Use the space below to note the names of any people you find it really difficult to get on with. (Note: you will not be showing this to anyone else so you can be honest!) Now try to write something positive about them (something of God's image in them). If you can't, then pray that you will see God's image somewhere in them in your contact with them this week or month.

Name   The aspect of God's image that I see

_____

_____

_____

going further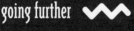

I Genesis 9:5,6 warns of the dangers of devaluing the image of God in our fellow man. List the ways we may be in danger of devaluing God's image in others today (whether Christians or not). How can we as Christians help guard against these dangers?

2 Which of the following activities do you feel help to further God's command to man to subdue/rule the earth?

– wildlife conservation pressure groups
– factory farming
– becoming a vegetarian
– making use of the earth's resources, ie coal.
– growing your own crops
– organic farming

• joining anti-GM food groups
• growing things (eg trees, livestock) for a purpose
• supporting 'save-the-badger' campaigns
• eating less
• keeping pets

Can you identify any ways in which you (or your group) could be more obedient to God's command?

CHILDREN OF GOD

AIM: to examine what it means to be God's children and what sort of Father God is.

NOTES FOR LEADERS

PRAYER/WORSHIP IDEAS

Songs and hymns
Choose some songs or hymns that focus particularly on our relationship with God the Father:

Great is Your Faithfulness
I have heard so many songs (The Father's Song)
Father God, I wonder
I'm your child

During the meeting
Find a large roll of wallpaper and fasten it to the wall. Provide newspapers and scissors and ask the group to cut out articles which give us a glimpse of the image of God in people. For example, an article of someone who went out of their way to help a neighbour, demonstrating compassion or somebody who's invented a new gadget, demonstrating creativity. Stick all the articles on the wallpaper and then give thanks for what you find.

Closing prayer
Pray together about any of the needs that have been mentioned in the My Story section.

ICEBREAKER
Explain to your group that today you will be thinking about what it means to be children of God. Just to get them into the right frame of mind, you're going to take them back to that most exciting of events when you're a child – a party! Have a couple of party games ready which will just be fun to do and will get everyone relaxing and laughing together. Ideas might include:

Pin the tail on the donkey: Each blindfolded person takes it in turns to try to pin the tail in the right place on a picture of a donkey.

Slice the cake: make a 'flour cake' by packing flour tightly into a pudding basin and then turning it out onto a tray. Place a cherry on top, provide a knife and get each person to slice away bits of the 'cake'. See how much of the 'cake' you can slice away without the cherry falling. The person who causes the cherry to fall must pick it out of the flour with their teeth.

Penny waddle: Place a small bowl on the floor a few metres away from the starting line. Two players each place a coin between their knees and race to waddle to the bowl and try to drop the coin into it. You could form 2 small teams and do this as a relay race.

BIBLE READING
1 John 2:28 – 3:3, 9, 10

RELATIONAL BIBLE STUDY
In Question 3 it is important to get people to try to explore why their picture of God as Father is the way it is. For some it may relate to their experience of their human father when they were young.

IN DEPTH
In Question 3, after people have shared the item circled, ask them to share how they have experienced this aspect of God's character.

MY STORY
This is an opportunity to share some of the needs in our lives. Again, if your group isn't used to this, encourage them gently by going first yourself. Encourage people to

listen carefully to each other as they share responses to Question 2. If sharing with the whole group would take too long or be overpowering for people, divide into threes or fours for Question 3. Encourage people to talk about the background to their needs before they turn to prayer. Question 4 is a way of affirming the group life as a whole, not just individuals in it. As leader, listen to what is said as it may give you some idea about the quality of group life.

GOING FURTHER
If you decide to tackle Question 1 in the group, share the workload by dividing into twos; give each pair two or three passages to study, as necessary.

Things to remember ...

notes on the Bible verses

1 John 2:28 – 3:3, 9, 10

2:28 John attaches great importance to this injunction to continue in close communion with Christ, by adding the appeal, *dear children*. He is aware that in the time leading to the end of the world, the going will get tough for Christians; we shall need great endurance. This encouragement to persevere forms the context of our passage.

The Christian's confidence at the time of judgement is that we are true offspring of God, and have lived as such.

2:29 – 3:1, 10 We become God's children through God's undeserved love, not through any virtue of our own. But right living and loving should be the evidence that we are his children: 'like father, like son'.

3:1–3, 9, 10 Human beings belong to one of two families: God's (marked by growing likeness to Jesus) or the devil's (otherwise known as 'the world', and marked by continuing sinfulness).

3:1,2 It is not yet 'obvious' to outsiders that Christians are God's children; nor was it self-evident to all onlookers that Jesus was the Son of God. Part of the glory of heaven is that when we see Jesus, we will reflect his likeness perfectly.

3:9,10 These sentences sound too 'black and white' for comfort; but John is not saying that Christins will *never* sin (compare 1 John 1:8–10). The key is in the phrasing, '*continue* to sin' and '*go on* sinning'. When someone becomes a Christian and is born into God's family, God's seed (or new life) in them is such a powerful reality that it smothers the habitual tendency to sin. Doing right and loving our brother become our increasingly normal behaviour, even though we are still far from perfect.

CHILDREN OF GOD

BIBLE READING
I John 2:28 – 3:3,9,10

RELATIONAL BIBLE STUDY

I Thinking back to your own childhood, what do you remember as the most important privileges and the biggest problems of being a child? (Underline 2 privileges, circle 2 problems.)

a limited responsibility
b lack of worries
c bedtime
d going to church
e school dinners
f being punished
g having food and clothes provided for you
h having fun
i kisses from relations

j unhappy relationships
k dressing up in best clothes
l holidays
m thoughtful, kind parents
n treats and surprises
o fights and quarrels
p don't remember any privileges
q other _____
r other _____

2 How do you feel about being one of God's children? (Underline any that apply.)

a I'm too old to be considered a child.
b It's great having a father who really understands me.
c I'm scared when I do something wrong.
d I wish he'd pay me more attention.
e I'd like a room of my own and to be left in peace on occasions.
f He expects too much of me.
g 'Over the moon' when he shows he loves me.
h Mystified because I don't understand him.
i Other _____

3 How do you picture God when you think of him as Father? Tick the one that best represents how you see his fatherhood. (If you wish, write or draw your own picture/character to sum up God's fatherhood.)

a school teacher
b policeman
c prison officer
d friendly old man

e PE instructor
f wise thinker
g a good Dad

IN DEPTH

I How do we know who the children of God are (3:9,10)? Circle the appropriate letter(s).

a They are all human beings.
b They call themselves Israelites.
c They are all those who love other people.
d They are obviously sinless.

e They exhibit God's 'family likeness'.
f They memorise important Bible passages.
g Other _____

2 How would you argue the value of being a child of God to someone who didn't consider him/herself a Christian?

a God takes the responsibilities for living off your shoulders.

b God ensures you'll come to no harm.

c One day you'll see him face to face.

d One day you will be like the Father.

e God will help you to live free of sin.

f You can love other people more effectively

g You were meant to be God's child and you've no real value or purpose until you acknowledge it.

h Other _____

MY STORY

I In what way do you feel you are most like a child of God at the moment? (Circle the most appropriate letter.)

a generally open and obedient to his will

b enjoying the good things he has supplied

c revelling in his love

d appreciating his forgiving nature

e accepting his discipline

f patiently waiting for his advice and direction

g other _____

2 Our heavenly Father provides for our needs as his children. Look at the list below and circle any that are current needs for you.

a to know that you are loved

b to receive advice/guidance on a specific issue

c to be valued for who you are

d to share particular burdens

e to know you are forgiven

f to have a shoulder to cry on

g to be freed to have fun

h other _____

3 Share with others in your group any need circled above, and spend some time praying for each other.

going further

I The Israelites were called the children of God (Deuteronomy 14:1). In what ways does their relationship with God (as seen in the Old Testament stories) mirror our relationship with God as Christians? Use the references below to summarise the ups and downs of that relationship. (If you have time, use a concordance or your memory to add other Old Testament stories which compare and contrast with the way God handles his children in the New Testament.)

Exodus 6:1–9 Exodus 16:1–3,11–30
Deuteronomy 9:1–6 Exodus 13:17 – 14:4
Exodus 19:3–8 Joshua 24:19–27

Exodus 14:10–29 Deuteronomy 4:32–40
Judges 3:7–11 Exodus 15:1–18
Deuteronomy 7:1–16 I Samuel 8:1–9, 19–22

2 It has been said that 'Man is not sure who he is because he has lost contact with the one who gives him identity and meaning'. How does becoming God's child help us to answer the following questions:

• Who am I?
• How should I live?
• What is my role in life?
• What is my eternal destiny?

'NOBODY'S PERFECT'

AIM: to look at the effects of sin on the world today, and to give group members the chance to focus on the effect of sin in their own lives in a way that can bring healing and forgiveness.

NOTES FOR LEADERS

PRAYER/WORSHIP IDEAS

Songs and hymns
Use songs or hymns that focus on the fact that the cross brings reconciliation, healing and forgiveness to us:

God of grace
He has clothed us in his righteousness
I am a new creation
Before the throne of God above

During the meeting
You might like to provide an opportunity for people to privately confess to God any issues thrown up by the meeting that they know they need to ask forgiveness for. Provide pens and small pieces of paper and, to the background of some instrumental music, suggest that people write down these things on pieces of paper, tear or scrunch them up and throw them in the bin. When everyone has done so, read the words of 1 John 1:8,9 and 2:1,2.

ICEBREAKER
We all know the imperfections in those close to us. They tend to be the things that irritate and annoy us. Often they are the small things – when he leaves clothes on the floor or she spends hours gabbing on the phone to her mother!

In fours, get each person in turn to mime their 'niggle' (something that really irritates them) with the others trying to guess what is happening.

BIBLE READING
Genesis 3:1–24

RELATIONAL BIBLE STUDY
In Question 2 try to encourage people to think openly and honestly about how they feel talking about sin. Why do they feel the way they do? And how does it affect their willingness to talk to others about Christianity?

IN DEPTH
Question 1 is an encouragement to see sin not just as an issue of personal morality, but as something that affects social structures and the rest of creation. Those who focus on personal issues alone in their answer may need to be challenged to a broader view of the effects of sin.

MY STORY
Decide whether you want people to answer Question 1 or 2 or both; and whether you think they would be willing to share their answers together. If so, put them in twos or threes. With either question, do not allow this to become a time to boast ('Look what I'm prepared to reveal.'). And help people who do not wish to share to know that this is perfectly all right.

Whether or not you have had group sharing, it is important to move on to a time of prayer. This could be silent, general prayer, guided by you; or, if there has been sharing, the small groups could pray for each other, perhaps placing hands on the head or shoulders of each one they pray for, to express their love and support. With prayer for forgiveness, it is good to read first some declaration of God's readiness to forgive, such as 1 John 1:7–10. In the case of prayer for healing or endurance, it is the author's view that God does heal us from all kinds of unwholeness, some things instantly, sometimes gradually, sometimes not till the next life. Therefore, instant healing isn't our right to demand. Because of sin in the world, a certain amount of suffering is part of the human condition. If this becomes controversial in the group and there isn't time to explain it fully, suggest another occasion when the topic can be explored more extensively.

GOING FURTHER

Question 2 would be ideal for any who find sin a difficult topic to discuss – this may be due to their own feelings of guilt which they cannot face. Tackle this question as part of the session if you think it will help people to get sin in its right place, and if you feel you have the resources to provide counsel in any cases of distress. You may need to help people distinguish between real guilt – God and our consciences accusing us of sins we have committed – and false guilt feelings. The latter often arise from something in our background telling us that something neutral (eg owning the latest labour-saving luxury item) or cultural (eg attending church only once on a Sunday) is sinful.

notes on the Bible verses

 Genesis 3:1–24

Man was not made as a sinful being. Sin resulted from a combination of man's freedom to act in the way he wished, and temptation from outside (3:1–6). The essence of sin was to disobey God's command (3:3); some Christians equate sin with sex, but God's call to multiply came before the Fall (Genesis 1:28).

Even this first sin was not the act of one isolated individual, but included one person influencing another (3:6). Sin is rarely limited to the one who perpetrates the sin (3:9–13). It often has a ripple effect, affecting others in its consequences (3:15, compare Exodus 20:5). So sin is not just a personal issue; it also permeates society and the whole human environment (3:17–19), corrupting politics, judicial systems, economic policies, etc.

Although the punishment for sin ordained by God is death (3:3; also 2:17) he does, even at this moment of the 'Fall', give man hope for the future:

- he doesn't abandon them, but continues to talk to them (3:8 and following);
- he limits their life but doesn't terminate it immediately (3:19);
- despite being under the curse of God's punishment, the man and woman still love each other, and will produce children and food (3:16–20);
- God makes them clothes, protecting them to some extent from the harshness of the world they are about to enter (3:21);
- he allows their newly-gained knowledge of good and evil to remain, although he does not (yet) give them eternal life (3:22–24).

Although suffering and pain are a general result of sin in a fallen world (3:16–19), it is clear from Jesus' teaching that not all the suffering and pain we experience is a direct result of our own sinfulness (see John 9:1–3). This leads to the controversial question of healing, which some today feel should be expected by all Christians who are ill or who suffer in some way. Other Bible passages have a bearing on this, but the perspective of this Genesis passage is that suffering and pain are experiences that, to some extent, we have to expect and possibly accept as the result of living in a sinful world.

'NOBODY'S PERFECT'

BIBLE READING
Genesis 3:1–24

RELATIONAL BIBLE STUDY

I What is sin? (Underline any appropriate answers.)

a playing with snakes
b being selfish
c over-eating
d something too serious to joke about
e disobeying God

f liking apples!
g knowing good and evil
h being afraid of God
i losing your innocence
j other _____

Can you attempt a group definition of the word 'sin'?

_____

_____

2 How would you feel about talking to a non-Christian friend or neighbour about 'sin'?

a Embarrassed: desperately searching for another word to use instead of sin.
b Guilty: because of their knowledge of your imperfection.
c Earnest: because of your concern for the effects of sin on their lives.
d Uncomfortable: as you don't really think it's a suitable topic to discuss with a neighbour.
e Worried: about being labelled a fanatic.
f Eager: to have the chance to point out where they're going wrong.
g Other _____

IN DEPTH

I Which of the following do you think result from sin in the world? (Put a tick by as many items as you like.)

a earthquakes and volcanoes
b lions killing antelopes
c old age
d marriage breakdown
e crime
f occult practice
g failing exams
h getting angry

i sex
j different church denominations
k famine in Africa
l Communism
m poverty
n tooth decay
o pain and suffering
p hard work.

2 What do you think is the worst effect of sin today? (Underline just one of the following.)

a people don't know God
b crime and evil in the world
c death and decay
d injustice in society

e pain and suffering
f lack of hope for the future
g other _____

MY STORY

1 God offers us forgiveness for our sins. Are there areas of your own life now where you need to seek his forgiveness? Think through the list below. Write anything appropriate after one or more items on the list. You need not share what you write down if you would prefer not to.

In my relationship with God: _____

In my own thoughts/attitudes/feelings:_____

In my relationships with those close to me:_____

In my work life:_____

In my leisure/social life:_____

2 Suffering and pain may not be a direct result of our personal sinfulness, but may be something we have to endure as a result of sin in the world. Is there any aspect of your life in which you are experiencing pain or suffering, and in which you need healing or at least the strength to endure? Identify the pain and then indicate in what way this group could help you (eg by praying for me, by doing my shopping, by not interfering, by babysitting, etc).

Painful areas:	This group could help by:
physical suffering: _____	_____
emotional struggles _____	_____
painful relationships _____	_____
issues that are painful to think through _____	_____
other pain or suffering in any aspect of life _____	_____

going further

1 Your closest friend discloses that he/she has been involved in one of the activities listed below. Put a tick against the two items that would shock you the most:

stealing a car
swearing
cheating at a game
fiddling income tax
shoplifting
telling lies
forging someone's signature
taking drugs

having an affair
taking stationery supplies from the office

Do you have a scale of wrongdoing, ie seeing some things as worse than others? Does the Bible categorise sin in this way?

2 Sin often leads to a sense of guilt (3:8–10). Real guilt (as opposed to baseless guilt-feelings) can be both a help and a hindrance in our

Christian discipleship. Make two lists, one of any positive ways that guilt can encourage our growth as Christians; the other of ways guilt can stunt it. Explore your own experience of guilt and identify any times when guilt has had a positive or negative effect on you.

THE COMPLETE MAN

AIM: to see Jesus as the model human being, and to take steps to become more whole as humans ourselves. We will be looking at the hope for mankind now, on earth. The next study will look at our future hope.

NOTES FOR LEADERS

PRAYER/WORSHIP IDEAS

Songs and hymns
Choose some songs or hymns that focus on Jesus.

We bow down
Lord, you have my heart
My Jesus, my Saviour
All heaven declares

Use Philippians 2:1–11 as a springboard for group praise. Encourage your group to contribute short sentence prayers of praise and adoration.

During the meeting
Get hold of some artistic representations of Jesus – perhaps from some library books of famous paintings. What do you think that the artist was trying to convey about Jesus through his art? Use any new insights in praise and thanksgiving.

ICEBREAKER
Before the session, find 10 well-known advertisements in colour magazines and cut away some familiar part of the picture – it doesn't have to be the product itself but something well-known that accompanies it, such as the slogan or trade mark. Paste the ads to cards, number them and stick them round the room so that participants can wander around and see them. Have paper and pencil for each group member to write on. Ask them to write down what is missing from each picture. At the end, compare answers and talk about how easy it is to recognise what is missing from familiar pictures. Explain that we are now going to look at our picture of Jesus and reconcile it to the one we find in the Bible.

BIBLE READING
Hebrews 2:5–18; Philippians 3:10–14

RELATIONAL BIBLE STUDY
Questions 1 and 2 focus on our changing image of Jesus. Encourage group members to think hard before they answer so that their answer, especially to Question 2, is an accurate reflection of their thought. Question 4 begins to explore the areas that will be shared in My Story; you may prefer not to spend time sharing them now.

IN-DEPTH BIBLE STUDY
The whole of this section looks at our potential for the future. You may want to focus on one or two questions, and to encourage a more thorough sharing of what group members have written down.

MY STORY

GOING FURTHER
Unless you have a group which knows the Bible exceptionally well, these questions will be more realistically tackled as homework. If people report their answers to the group later, give them time to share their feelings about whichever question they have done.

notes on the Bible verses

 Hebrews 2:5–18

2:5 The *world to come* is the new age of salvation heralded by Christ's life, death and glorification. Although its fulfilment will be in the future, Christians have already entered it; and Jesus is Lord of it.

2:6–9 The author quotes from Psalm 8, which celebrates the glory of man as God's 'deputy' on earth. But only Jesus truly lived up to this calling; he took on the mantle of 'man as he should have been'. From one point of view, the perfect and ideal man did not need, and certainly did not deserve, to die. But Jesus did suffer death – partly to identify with the full range of human experience, but even more to endure the spiritual death penalty for everyone's sins, so releasing us from the power and fear of death (2:14,15) and bringing us to glory with him (2:10).

2:10,11 These verses describe two processes of 'perfecting'. On the one hand, there is the 'salvation' of Christians. Many think of this as meaning simply 'saved from the consequences of my sins'. In fact, in the Bible salvation means 'health' or 'wholeness', and relates to God's work of renewing man and restoring him to his creation glory, complete and unmarred by sin. Salvation is a process that begins with submission to the crucified and risen Jesus, continues throughout our earthly lives as we are gradually 'made holy' (more like the perfect Man), and culminates in our own glorification when we go, finally made perfect, to live with God. In this session we are concentrating on the middle stage of the process: the way we are changing or can change now as we seek God's salvation in our lives today. (For a whole course on this growth in wholeness, see the BODYBUILDERS book *Growing through Change – seizing the opportunities life gives you.*)

More surprising than the idea that we need to be made perfect is the statement in 2:10 that God made Jesus perfect through suffering. This does not refer to moral improvement; Jesus was already the perfect Man. It means the necessary qualification to become our perfect *author of salvation*. Only by suffering death (physical and spiritual) could he save us from death.

2:14–18: Jesus is the perfect liberator – he sets us free from all that prevents us from being whole: in particular, the devil, who tries to tempt us and frighten us. Not only has he atoned for our sins, thus removing the barrier to God's presence; he has experienced the devil's attacks and conquered them, so that he can sympathise and help. And remember, the Hebrew mind saw the person as a unity, not clearly divided into body, mind and spirit. So the wholeness that Jesus brings is over every aspect of our lives.

Philippians 3:10–14

This glimpse of Paul's ambitions is a model for humanity made new in Christ.

3:10,11 The heart of the matter is increasingly to know Jesus and to become 'wrapped up' in his life. In detail this means appropriating the power of God which raised Jesus from the grave, to live more and more in tune with God's will. In turn this will expose us to sharing the inner pain and outward opposition, which Jesus continues to feel in the struggle to win mankind over to God's kingdom. Sooner or later (and at the time of writing, Paul expected it sooner) we shall die and trust to be resurrected to heaven. In such experience, Jesus has gone before us and comes with us.

3:12,13 We do not reach perfection in this life. The permanent stance for renewed humanity is *press on*.

3:13,14 Paul repeats his motto and emblem in the picture of running a race. God's call for 'whole' human beings is to race towards the finishing tape (*goal*), with the energy that wins gold medals (*prize*).

THE COMPLETE MAN

BIBLE READING
Hebrews 2:5–13; Philippians 3:10–14

RELATIONAL BIBLE STUDY

I *We see Jesus* (Hebrews 2:9). Which of the following descriptions best sums up your childhood picture of Jesus? (Circle the letter that comes closest to your memory.)

a a gentle lamb resting peacefully in the meadow

b an ordinary man like the person across the road

c a superhuman hero flying to the aid of all in need

d a mysterious cloaked figure walking in the shadows

e a tall blond man with a beard

f a confusing person – sometimes like a man and sometimes like God

g other _____

2 How do you picture Jesus now?

_____

_____

3 Jesus shared in our humanity; he was *like his brothers in every way* (Hebrews 2:14,17). What feature of his humanity do you most appreciate? Give each of the following a score out of 6 (6 indicates your highest appreciation).

a his ability to overcome temptation

b his humility – like a servant

c his ability to cry when sad

d his stamina in walking vast distances to meet people

e his ability to suffer and to experience pain

f his childhood and his need to learn

g his desire to meet and help the disadvantaged in society

h other _____

4 What aspects of your humanity are you happy with and glad to talk to Jesus about as your brother (Hebrews 2:11), and what aspects would you rather keep private from him? Take the items listed below and write those you would share with him in the visible portion of the iceberg and the others in the submerged portion.

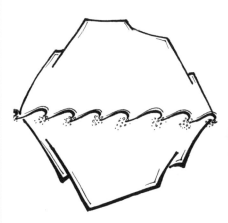

my love life   my job/career
my physical appearance   my social life
my wisdom   my leisure pursuits
my family life

IN DEPTH

I How do you react to each of these descriptions (from Hebrews 2) of you as a member of the human race?

* *made a little lower than the angels* (v 7)
* *crowned with glory and honour* (v 7)
* *everything put under your feet* (v 8)
* *Jesus' brother or sister* (vs 11, 12)

2 Try to think of ways in which you have felt or experienced these privileges (eg for *everything under your feet* you might remember watching a plane take off and being amazed at man's mastery of technology).

Description   **Examples**

made a little lower than the angels _____

crowned with glory and honour _____

everything under your feet _____

Jesus' brother or sister _____

3   Paul talks about pressing on towards the goal (Philippians 3:14). What was Paul's goal here,
and do you think he had others? What are your goals in life? Jot down a list of Paul's goals
and your goals:

Paul's goals   My goals

_____

_____

MY STORY

I   God wants to see his wholeness (equivalent to glory, salvation, holiness and freedom, see
Hebrews 2:10,11,15) in every area of our lives.

job/career	hobbies/interests	wisdom
physical health	church life	values
ambitions/hope	emotions	lifestyles
friendships	family life	this group

Can you identify any of the following 'symptoms of unwholeness' in any area of your life?
unhealthy feelings (U); dishonouring God (D); lack of enjoyment (L); dishonesty (H); lack of
fulfilment (F); incompleteness (I); lack of satisfaction (S); Other ( ).
Mark items in the list with letters as appropriate. Spend time thinking about the ways you
feel you lack God's wholeness in these areas.

2   Choose two areas from the list in Question I that you would like to do something about.
Then try to identify anything you or your group can do to bring increasing wholeness to
that area.

Area 1: _____   **Area 2:** _____

I could: _____   I could: _____

_____   _____

This group could: _____   This group could: _____

_____

going further ∿

I   Make a thorough study of
Mark's Gospel, and list all
the ways in which Jesus
reveals his solidarity with
the human race.

2   *Salvation* (Hebrews 2:10)
means, in essence, health or
wholeness. Use a
concordance to look at the
places where this word is
used in the New Testament,
and try to build up a more
detailed picture of its
meaning.

3   What part do we have to
play and what part does
God's Spirit play in achieving
our salvation/wholeness?
Start with Philippians
3:10–14; then consult
Philippians 2:12,13 and
Ephesians 2:4–10.

THERE'S MORE TO LIFE THAN DEATH

AIM: to allow everyone to examine their attitudes to death and their feelings about immortality.

NOTES FOR LEADERS

During this session, we focus on death. If there are members who have recently suffered bereavement, you may like to see them earlier in the week and explain the topic for study, giving them the opportunity to opt out if they are not at a point where they can cope.

PRAYER/WORSHIP IDEAS

Songs and hymns

Choose songs or hymns that help the group to focus on the hope which God gives us for the future.

There's a place (Because of You)
Soon and very soon
Nothing can separate us from the love of God
My first love (Like a child)

Closing prayer

You will need a couple of seeds for each member of the group (sunflower or mustard and cress seeds will work best) and yoghurt pots filled with earth. Give the seeds out and, as people hold them in their hands and consider them, read 1 Corinthians 15:35–44 out loud. Ask those who would like to do so to plant their seeds in a pot as a symbol of offering their life to God to use as he will, and of their Christian hope in the resurrection of the body and everlasting life. Suggest that as they take them home and watch their seeds grow, that they thank God for their hope for the future.

ICEBREAKER

Have pencils and identical pieces of paper ready.

BIBLE READING

1 Corinthians 15:12–22 35–44

RELATIONAL BIBLE STUDY

Question 2 may prove hard or upsetting for some to answer. Allow people to pass it if they can't answer. If some want to answer but seem to struggle to get out the words, allow them time – don't rush them. If anyone gets upset, don't ignore it; coping with tears in a session is important. One way of helping a tearful group member is to move next to them and to place a hand on their arm or shoulder to show that you care (someone else in your group may do this automatically). If they are in the middle of talking, ask them quietly if they want to continue or whether they've no more to say. Stay close, and if they continue to be upset ask them privately if they would like to talk about it after the session.

IN DEPTH

For Question 4, have pencils, crayons and blank paper ready. Encourage people to draw using symbols and colours to represent their thoughts. Reassure them that thoughts aren't necessarily tidy and you're not after a masterpiece! Those who feel that they really can't draw can be encouraged to put some squiggles on paper as long as it means something which they can explain to the rest.

MY STORY

The questions are based on the idea that God wants us to live life to the full (John 10:10). Questions 1 and 2 encourage people to identify areas in which they have more living to do. Question 1 is a reflection on the Relational Bible Study; don't linger on it if you discussed that fully.

GOING FURTHER

Question 3 is one way of encouraging group members to share some of the exciting aspects of their faith. There is always the possibility of inviting any interested interviewees to a special open group time to explore more.

Things i've learned leading this group ...

N.B. Which Bodybuilders title shall i use next?

notes on the Bible verses

I Corinthians 15:12–22, 35–44

There were people in Corinth who denied that the dead could be raised, and argued that death was 'the final curtain' for everyone. The importance of Jesus' final resurrection to Paul is evident from the pains he takes to argue how fundamental it is to Christianity.

15:12–19 Here is a summary of Paul's reasoned argument for the resurrection:

If resurrection from the dead is not real,

1 Jesus is still dead (v13,16);
2 the Christian way of life is pointless (v14,17);
3 all the apostles and Christian teachers who teach a resurrection are lying (v15);
4 we cannot go to heaven (v18,19).

15:20 Jesus' resurrection is proof that others will also be raised.

15:21,22 Here Paul makes the link between Adam, through whom mortality came into the world, and Jesus, who brings again the chance of immortality. This is what God has intended for mankind since the beginning of time. The verses do not teach that all human beings, regardless of Christian faith, will receive eternal life; it is all *in Christ* who will be made alive. All of us are born 'into Adam', with the death sentence hanging over us. Those who are 'born again', into Christ, are born into his quality of life, that is, eternal life.

15:35–44 Paul explains that just as the seed is transformed when it 'dies', into a plant, so death is the point of transformation for man. In explaining what happens to the body at resurrection, he uses a number of pictures from the natural world. In summary, Paul is saying that we will have a body after the resurrection which in many respects will be different from (and better than) our present body. Yet the new will be a development and fulfilment of the old, not a different species altogether. From the accounts of Jesus' appearances it would seem that our bodies will remain human in form; and recognisably 'us', even if not at first glance!

THERE'S MORE TO LIFE THAN DEATH

ICEBREAKER
How would you like to be known by those you leave behind after your death? Write your own anonymous epitaph on a piece of paper starting 'Here lies... who...'(leave your name blank). Fold your piece of paper and place it in the centre of the floor or table, then pick up one that doesn't belong to you. Take it in turns to read them out. The group should guess the name of the person they think it applies to. At the end of the exercise, reveal whether your epitaph was correctly identified.

BIBLE READING
I Corinthians 15:12–22, 35–44

RELATIONAL BIBLE STUDY
I *This life* (15:19). How satisfied are you with your life at present? (Mark a cross on the scale between the two extremes to indicate your feelings.)

Life? Don't talk
to me about life! _____

This is the life –
fantastic!

2 *Fallen asleep in Christ* (15:18). If the topic of your own death were to arise in a conversation, how would you react?

a Talk quite naturally and matter-of-factly, without feeling anything in particular.
b Feel sick in the pit of your stomach and fight back the tears.
c Change the subject as quickly as you can.
d Express your delight at the thought of living in heaven.
e Pretend to be unconcerned but cover up your real uncertainty.
f Other _____

3 How do you feel about life for ever with God?

a Great!
b It's too remote to think about.
c I actually have my doubts about it.
d Boring, boring, boring.

e I hope I'll be able to do what I like!
f There's too much to worry about in this life.
g I'm waiting patiently.
h Other _____

IN DEPTH
I Paul suggests a number of consequences that follow if the idea of resurrection is false. Tick all those below that figure in his reasoning. Underline the one that you find most disturbing. It means that:

a Christians have been lying.
b no one will be saved from death.
c this life is all there is.
d Christians are living and working under an illusion.

e our sins are still all unforgiven.
f death will be a painful experience.
g those who are already dead have no hope.

2 If a non-Christian asked you *How are the dead raised?* (15:35), how would you reply? Use the explanation given in verses 37–44 to put together a reply. Write it below:

_____

_____

3 At the resurrection, our bodies are going to be different. What are you looking forward to most about your new body? (Circle the most important item for you.)

a No more decay or weakness (filled teeth, aches and pains, tiredness, etc).

b No more sinful instincts to do wrong rather than right.

c No more physical limitations.

d Never having to die.

e Other(s) _____

4 How do you picture eternal life? On a blank sheet of paper, draw some pictures that represent any of the thoughts, fantasies, questions or concerns you have about what life will be like after the resurrection. Share these and talk about them in your group.

MY STORY

1 Reflecting on this session so far, is there anything in your attitude to

a life on earth at present or **b** death, that you feel is unhelpful or that you're not happy with? Share it with the group and talk about how you would like to change that attitude.

2 Is there anything still unfinished in your life that you would like to complete before you die? Use the following categories to guide your thinking.

Ambitions; Work; Relationships; Family; Making up for your wrongdoings; Specific work for God; Other(s)

Share with the rest of the group one thing that you would seriously like to give time to, and together look at ways you can begin to work at it. Write down one practical step that you can take this week.

going further

1 Spend time thinking about your attitudes to death, thinking back over any past experiences of bereavement. How do you reconcile the feelings of sadness, anger and despair commonly experienced in bereavement with the Christian belief in the resurrection and afterlife?

2 Make a study of these passages on Jesus' resurrection and the life to come, in order to build a picture of the future for mankind:

John 20–21; Acts 1:1–11; 1 Corinthians 15; 2 Corinthians 5:1–10; 1 Thessalonians 4:13–5:11.

3 Next time you're having coffee with or out for a drink with one or two close friends, how about asking them what they think about death and the hereafter and even what they think most other people in our society think about it? For example, why do they think death is such a difficult subject? Do they ever think about their own death? What do they think of the Christian claim that Jesus rose from the dead and how do they react to the idea of eternal life, ie for ever and ever?

'Does your Bible study deal with the issues that friends are talking about at the pub or in the office?'

If you want to talk to your friends about why the Bible is relevant to what they are into, these are the Bible studies for you.
Mike Pilavachi, Soul Survivor

A great way to explore up-to-date issues and concerns in the light of the Bible.
Rev Dr Michael Green, Advisor in Evangelism to the Archbishops of Canterbury and York

How can you engage with friends and colleagues as they discuss best-selling novels, chart music, pop culture TV shows or Oscar-nominated films?

CONNECT can help – innovative, creative and thought-provoking Bible studies for groups available as an electronic download or in print.

Titles available

- Billy Elliot
- The Matrix
- Harry Potter
- TV Game Shows
- Chocolat
- How to be Good
- U2: All that you can't leave behind

With more coming soon

Available from all good Christian bookshops
from www.scriptureunion.org.uk
from Scripture Union Mail Order: PO Box 5148, Milton Keynes MLO, MK2 2YX
Tel 01908 856006
or as an electronic download from www.connectbiblestudies.com

connect Bible Studies are jointly produced by Scripture Union, Premier Media Group and Damaris Trust.